25/14
$ 16.75

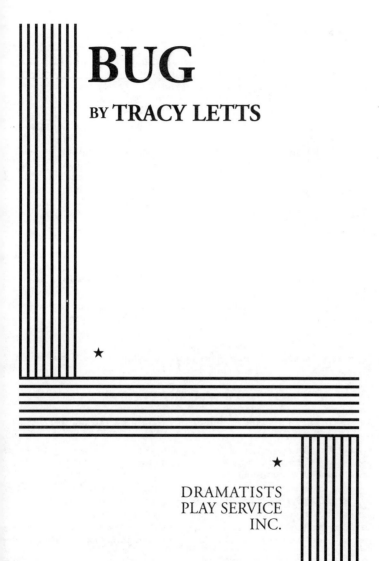

BUG

BY **TRACY LETTS**

★

★

DRAMATISTS
PLAY SERVICE
INC.

BUG
Copyright © 2005, Tracy Letts

All Rights Reserved

SPECIAL NOTE

Originally produced Off-Broadway
by Scott Morfee, Amy Danis and Mark Johannes.

For Holly

BUG received its world premiere at the Gate Theatre in London, England, opening in September 1996. It was directed by Wilson Milam. The cast was as follows:

AGNES WHITE .... Shannon Cochran
R.C. .... Holly Wantuch
PETER EVANS .... Michael Shannon
JERRY GOSS .... Marc A. Nelson
DR. SWEET .... Jeff Still

BUG was produced at the Barrow Street Theatre (Amy Danis, Mark Johannes and Scott Morfee, Producers) in New York City, opening on February 29, 2004. It was directed by Dexter Bullard; the set design was by Lauren Helpern; the lighting design was by Tyler Micoleau; the sound design was by Brian Ronan; the costume design was by Kim Gill; the production manager was Brian Duea; and the production stage manager was Richard A. Hodge. The cast was as follows:

AGNES WHITE .... Shannon Cochran
R.C. .... Amy Landecker
PETER EVANS .... Michael Shannon
JERRY GOSS .... Michael Cullen
DR. SWEET .... Reed Birney

CHARACTERS

AGNES WHITE, 44 years old
R. C. (RONNIE)
PETER EVANS, 27 years old
JERRY GOSS, early 40s
DR. SWEET

PLACE

A motel room on the outskirts of Oklahoma City.

TIME

The present.

BUG

ACT ONE

PROLOGUE

Lights fade up to a dim glow on Agnes. She stands in the open doorway of the motel room, staring into the night, smoking a cigarette, a little drunk, an empty wine glass in her hand. Radio salsa music drifts in from the room next door. Traffic drones monotonously on a nearby highway. A long, still moment. The phone rings. She sways to the bed, flops on it, answers the phone.

AGNES. 'Lo? *(Beat.)* Hello? *(Beat.)* Hello. *(Beat.)* Jerry? Is that you? *(Beat.)* Jerry? It's you, idn't it. You son of a bitch. *(She hangs up. She spots her waitress apron on the floor by the bed, grabs it, pulls out a wad of bills. After riffling through it, she drops the money in the bedside table drawer. She then carries the apron to a glass jug filled with loose change and dumps the change from the apron into the jug. She wraps up the apron, chucks it in the closet. She checks the air conditioner, flips a couple of switches. She bangs it with her fist and it rumbles into life. Agnes goes to her table, finds her empty wine battle, pitches it. Grabs an unopened bottle, searches for the corkscrew, finds it, opens the wine, searches for her glass, finds it on the bed, pours a drink. Talks to herself inaudibly. She collects dirty dishes, carries them to the bathroom. Runs water in the sink, throws in some soap, dumps the dishes in. Catches herself in the mirror, sees something she doesn't like, puts on lipstick. The phone rings again. She turns off the water, comes back to the living room, answers the phone.)* Hello? *(Beat.)* Fuck you. *(She hangs up. Talks to herself. The phone rings again. She answers it.)* Jerry? Where are you? Did you get out? *(Beat.)* You're gonna call me, you might

7

as well talk. All you do this way is freak me out. *(Beat.)* Fuck off, all right? I don't need this shit. Fuckin' hardleg. *(Beat.)* Hello? Jerry? *(Beat.)* Y'know I can call the cops. If they trace it to you, you're busted, you're in direct, y' know, whatever. *(Beat.)* I got a gun. *(She hangs up quickly. The phone rings again. She gets off the bed, crosses quickly to the door, shuts and locks it. She crosses back toward the bed, a couple of hesitant steps. She stares at the phone as it continues to ring. Lights fade out. In the blackout, country-and-western music.)*

Scene 1

Lights up on Agnes on the bed, smoking a rock of freebase out of a pipe. R.C. sits beside her, chopping and arranging six lines of cocaine with a razor blade. Country-and-western plays on the boom box.

AGNES. Fuck's he doin' here?
R.C. He's goin' to the party with me —
AGNES. Where'd he come from?
R.C. He was at the club —
AGNES. I don't know him, I don't know what shit he's into —
R.C. He's all right, he's just quiet —
AGNES. He's a fuckin' maniac, for all I know —
R.C. — he's harmless, he's just hangin' out —
AGNES. How do you know? You know him?
R.C. Hell, yes, I know him, of course I know him —
AGNES. He's a maniac DEA ax murderer, Jehovah's Witness —
R.C. Suckin' on that pipe like it's his momma's tit, probably safe to say he's not real high up in the DEA —
AGNES. Don't bring people here with you, R.C., I don't trust —
R.C. Go to this party with us.
AGNES. I'm too fucked up.
R.C. It's a *party,* for God's sake —
AGNES. I don't know any of those people.
R.C. You know me, you know Lavoice —
AGNES. You know what I mean —
R.C. You know Peter. Play your cards right, maybe you'll get bred.

8

AGNES. Don't even start —

R.C. You don't think he's good-lookin'?

AGNES. Ted Bundy was good-lookin' —

R.C. Ted Bundy's dead —

AGNES. — that German guy —

R.C. Don't tell me you don't wanna get laid —

AGNES. Gettin' laid is one thing —

AGNES.	R.C.
— wakin' up with my head missin' is somethin' else entirely.	— if you don't mind some sweaty mongoloid on top of you —

R.C. — but you do think he's good-lookin'. *(They crack up.)*

AGNES. I wish you'd come over more often.

R.C. You forget I got my significant trouble waitin' for me at home —

AGNES. Bring her over.

R.C. Ah, she's all worked up over this custody thing.

AGNES. How's that goin'?

R.C. Back in court, week from Friday. I don't think the state's too hot on reuniting children with their beautiful lesbian mothers.

AGNES. You could probably pick better places than Oklahoma to be a homo.

R.C. Like anybody ever picked it. She's not goin' anywhere, long as that little boy's here.

AGNES. I like Lavoice. She's a character —

R.C. You gotta like a woman who can fix your chopper —

R.C.	AGNES.
— but she might be a little jealous of you, tell the truth.	Seems like I used to know more characters a few years back.

AGNES. We used to have some characters down at the club. Now it's a buncha damn career women.

R.C. I don't think you can call menopause a career.

AGNES. Seems like any more, everyone I ever knew's married, or dead, or in prison.

R.C. Your rowdy friends settled down — ?

AGNES. I used to have a party myself ever' now and again —

R.C. We're havin' a party right now —

AGNES. No, I mean, like a barbecue —

R.C. Hey, this is the way you wanted it. You're the one hermitized yourself.

AGNES. You can't blame me for that.

R.C. That's a long time ago.

AGNES. He's been callin' again.

R.C. What's he want?

AGNES. He don't talk. He just breathes.

R.C. You sure it's him?

AGNES. Who else would it be?

R.C. Then you're not sure.

AGNES. It's him, I know it's him. Calls started right after he got out.

R.C. Get you a police whistle and blast it into the phone.

AGNES. I'm hopin' he'll just get bored.

R.C. You be careful. That's man's dangerous.

AGNES. I know it —

R.C. I can't believe they let him out. I figured he'd kill somebody in there, and they'd throw away the key. *(Yelling into bathroom.)* Hey, whyn'tcha give somebody else a chance?!

AGNES. I never been that lucky.

R.C. Don't you let him in, he comes back here. *(Peter enters from the bathroom. Agnes passes him the freebase pipe. During the following, he fixes the pipe, hits it. R.C. offers a rolled-up dollar bill to Agnes, who uses it to snort her lines.)*

AGNES.	PETER.
I hope he don't come by.	I'm not an ax murderer.

R.C. Wishful thinkin'.

AGNES. It's been two years.

R.C. He's callin', ain't he? It ain't like he forgot you.

AGNES. Right —

R.C. Get some bars on your windows maybe.

AGNES. You can just stand outside and throw peanuts at me.

R.C. Get an attack dog.

AGNES. I can take care of myself.

R.C. He won't be satisfied until he's —

AGNES.	PETER.
So I need to get an attack dog — ?	I'm not an ax murderer.

AGNES. I'm sorry, what? *(Agnes and R.C. share a look, then burst into laughter.)*

PETER. I'm not an ax murderer.

R.C. Can I use your phone?

AGNES. *(To R.C.)* Sure. *(To Peter.)* I didn't really think you were.

PETER. Okay.

AGNES. *(Re: cocaine.)* Here you go …
PETER. No, I — *(R.C. yells into the phone, trying to be heard over the sounds of a party at the other end of the line.)*

R.C.	PETER.
Hey, hello?! Who is this?! Who?! Is Lavoice there?! Lavoice! She's … she's got short … Hello?!	I don't snort it.
	AGNES.
Hey, I'm trying to find Lavoice! Lavoice! She's a big dike, all right?! Named Lavoice!	You was hittin' that pipe pretty good. *(Beat.)*
R.C. Hey, girl, what the fuck is goin' on over there?! It sounds like … ! *(Beat.)* I say it sounds like the end of the world! *(Laughs; beat.)* He said what now?! Speak up! *(Beat.)* Well, are you all right? *(Beat.)*	PETER. I know, I just don't like the powder. It's not healthy. *(Beat.)*
	AGNES. I didn't exactly have you pegged as the health nut type —
You tell him he lays another fuckin' hand on you, he's gonna have to deal with me! All right, then, I'm gettin' outta here! You gonna be there?! *(Beat.)* No, don't try to leave, I'm comin'! *(Beat.)*	PETER. You're very beautiful.
	AGNES. Huh?
	PETER. I said you're very beautiful.
All right, I'm on my way! I'll see you there! All right! Bye!	AGNES. Thank you.
	PETER. You're welcome.
	AGNES. Thank you.
	PETER. I'm sorry if I embarrassed you.

AGNES. I just don't take compliments very well. *(R.C. hangs up the phone.)*
R.C. I gotta get outta here. Some guy grabbed Lavoice, or squeezed somethin', and she slapped him and he threatened her or some shit.

I hate to eat 'n run, but —

AGNES. Don't worry. Listen, you have — ?

R.C. I got you all set up, Sister. (*R.C. gives Agnes a small glass vial of cocaine.*)

AGNES. Let me grab my —

R.C. I'll get it from you at work.

AGNES. You sure?

R.C. Yep. Let's saddle up, Johnny Depp.

PETER. I've changed my mind.

R.C. What's the matter?

PETER. Nothing. I'll just go from here. (*R.C. kisses Agrees good-night, brief, intimate.*)

AGNES. Will you call me?

R.C. I'll see you at work.

AGNES. Call me.

R.C. All right.

AGNES. You promise?

R.C. I'll call. We'll do something this week, okay? (*To Peter.*) Don't do anything I wouldn't do. (*R.C. darts out, pulling the door behind her. Agnes and Peter take each other in.*)

AGNES.	PETER.
You want one last drink?	I guess I'll go then.
(*Quick beat.*)	(*Quick beat.*)
I should get to bed	Yeah, I could have
anyway —	another Coke —

AGNES. Help yourself.

PETER. Thanks. (*Agnes tidies the room, dumping some empties, cleaning an ashtray. Peter gets a Coke from the fridge and wipes the top of the can with his shirt sleeve.*) You've known each other awhile.

AGNES. Few years, I guess.

PETER. I just met her tonight.

AGNES. Why'd you change your mind about the party?

PETER. I don't know. It just didn't seem like my cup of tea. (*He opens the Coke.*)

AGNES. Have a real drink, for Chrissake. People who don't drink make me nervous.

PETER. I make people nervous anyway. (*The air conditioner cuts off.*)

AGNES. Why's that?

PETER. 'Cause I pick up on things, I think. That makes people uncomfortable.

AGNES. Pick up on things.

PETER. Things not apparent.

AGNES. That's a talent.

PETER. Mm-hm.

AGNES. What do you pick up from me?

PETER. You're lonely. I know that much.

AGNES. Doesn't exactly make you Jeanne Dixon.

PETER. Who's Jeanne Dixon?

AGNES. She was … y'know, that psychic, told Teddy Kennedy that Jack'd get shot.

PETER. Oh. You live here?

AGNES. Yeah.

PETER. In the motel.

AGNES. Yeah.

PETER. That's weird.

AGNES. Why is that weird?

PETER. I don't know. *(Beat.)* Can I put on some more music?

AGNES. Yeah, sure. *(He goes to the boom box, puts on music. Agnes fixes the freebase pipe. She and Peter hit the pipe during the following.)* I get maid service. All my bills are paid, except the phone.

PETER. I didn't want to go.

AGNES. You didn't want to go. Where, to the — ?

PETER. I didn't want to leave. I just, I guess I'd just like to talk.

AGNES. Uh …

PETER. You're suspicious.

AGNES. Not particularly. I don't know you.

PETER. No, of course not.

AGNES. Anybody, really, comes into your place, a stranger —

PETER. No, I know what you mean. Because I'm suspicious, I think, that's my nature. But I'm trying to start something different.

AGNES. With me.

PETER. No, just … I don't mean to freak you out, I'm just trying to make a connection, or whatever.

AGNES. Right …

PETER. I'd like to see you again.

AGNES. How do you mean?

PETER. I mean … see you again, what I said.

AGNES. I don't, I don't know.

PETER. Okay, I —

AGNES. I don't party like this ever' night or nothin', so don't —

PETER. I just wanted to see you.

AGNES. Why?

13

PETER. Just … why people like to see each, other. Jesus, I don't want anything weird.

AGNES. 'Cause a man's the last thing I need.

PETER. I don't want to go to bed with you.

AGNES. Now don't butter me up or nothin'.

PETER. I'm not good for much anyway.

AGNES. What's that mean?

PETER. Women aren't really my bag.

AGNES. You a homo?

PETER. I'm not anything, really. I'm done with that. I'm just looking for a friend.

AGNES. You a con?

PETER. No, ma'am.

AGNES. Don't call me ma'am. Make me feel like your mother.

PETER. You're not old enough to be my mother.

AGNES. Good.

PETER. She's dead, anyway.

AGNES. Sorry.

PETER. She's been dead a long time.

AGNES. You don't even sound like you're from Oklahoma.

PETER. I'm from Beaver.

AGNES. Ah, well, we're all from Beaver — ain't we?

PETER. Pardon?

AGNES. Skip it.

PETER. Up in the Panhandle. My dad's a preacher up there.

AGNES. What church's he preach at?

PETER. He doesn't have a church.

AGNES. Where's he meet his congregation?

PETER. He doesn't have one, really.

AGNES. Huh. *(Peter examines her motel artwork: a large, brightly painted abstract, done in oil, possibly depicting a south-of-the-border street scene.)* First day I moved in here, I said I was gonna take that piece of shit down. I got to where I kind of like it.

PETER. Why?

AGNES. I dunno. It's kinda like "Margaritaville."

PETER. There's stuff in it.

AGNES. Stuff?

PETER. Hidden stuff.

AGNES. You mean, like a … what do you mean?

PETER. People and things. If you really look at it. *(She studies the painting.)* You have to look at it hard enough. You'll see it.

14

AGNES. That's weird.

PETER. Do you hear that?

AGNES. What? *(He turns off the stereo.)* I don't hear nothin'.

PETER. Listen. *(They listen. Silence.)*

AGNES. You're hearin' things. *(A high-pitched chirp. Another silence. Another chirp.)* Helskatoot.

PETER. What is that, is that — ?

AGNES. Goddamn cricket. *(Another chirp.)* Jesus … *(She looks for the cricket.)* Can you tell where it's comin' from?

PETER. Sounds like it's —

AGNES. Over here, right? *(Another chirp.)*

PETER. No, maybe it's … *(He helps her look for it.)*

AGNES. Don't kill him. It's bad luck.

PETER. Why is that, do you think?

AGNES. Some smart-ass cricket probably just made it up. *(Another chirp.)* It's in the bathroom.

PETER. Really? I thought —

AGNES. I'll bet it's … *(She goes into the bathroom.)*

PETER. Do you see it?

AGNES. No. *(Another chirp.)* Goddamnit —

PETER. It's out here. *(She reenters.)*

AGNES. Where?

PETER. I don't know. Up there. *(Another chirp.)*

AGNES. It's the smoke alarm. The battery's gone dead on the smoke alarm. *(She struggles with the smoke alarm.)* Can you get that off there? *(He struggles with the smoke alarm.)*

PETER. No. *(Another chirp.)*

AGNES. Then kill the son of a bitch. It's not bad luck to kill a smoke alarm.

PETER. I need something — *(She hands him a doo-dad. He whacks at the smoke detector a couple of times, knocks it off the wall.)*

AGNES. Success.

PETER. Success. You should get rid of that.

AGNES. Why?

PETER. They're dangerous. They've got americium-241 in them.

AGNES. What's that?

PETER. It's an element, a radioactive element.

AGNES. Jesus.

PETER. More radioactive than plutonium.

AGNES. Holy shit. No wonder I feel so lousy.

PETER. Yeah. Here … *(He exits the room, taking the smoke alarm*

15

with him.)

AGNES. What are you doin'?

PETER. *(As he goes.)* No, I'm just … *(She stands alone in the room, checks herself in the mirror. He reenters.)* Okay, then … I should go.

AGNES. Where do you live?

PETER. I'm kind of between addresses right now.

AGNES. What's that mean, you don't have a place?

PETER. No, I got a place I stay …

AGNES. Where?

PETER. Nowhere. Just … where I stay.

AGNES. You can stay here tonight, if you want. Sleep on the floor.

PETER. I don't want to put you out.

AGNES. Somebody on the floor while I'm asleep's not puttin' me out.

PETER. Okay. That'd be nice.

AGNES. It's just a floor.

PETER. Nice of *you*. *(She locks up, throws him a pillow and blanket. Peter puts his hand to his mouth, groans.)*

AGNES. What's the matter?

PETER. Tooth.

AGNES. There's aspirins in the medicine cabinet.

PETER. I'm okay. *(He makes a pallet on the floor. Agnes turns off the lights, strips out of her cut-offs and tank top, maybe allowing Peter to see her, maybe not. She gets in bed. Peter lays on the floor, on his back, fully dressed. The air conditioner comes on.)*

AGNES. What's the matter with the powder?

PETER. It's not healthy to just snort it like that. You need to cook it to get out the … stuff that's bad for you.

AGNES. What stuff's that?

PETER. Mm … just …

AGNES. I don't really think any of it's good for you.

PETER. Some things are worse than others. *(Blackout. In the blackout, sounds: air conditioner, traffic, garbage truck, running shower.)*

Scene 2

Lights rise on the following morning. Agnes lays in bed, just waking. The bathroom door is closed and the shower is running. A pot of coffee sits on the hot plate. Agnes has a coughing fit, rolls over to the bedside table, lights a smoke. The shower shuts off. A man whistles loudly in the bathroom.

AGNES.   *(Calling into bathroom.)* There should be some clean towels under the sink. *(Beat.)* Thanks for makin' the coffee. *(The door opens and Jerry Goss emerges from the steam-filled bathroom, wearing jeans, a towel draped around his neck.)*

GOSS.   You're welcome. *(Agnes is speechless. Goss goes about his business, putting his shirt on, combing his hair, pouring coffee.)* How do you stand that dinky li'l shower? I could hardly get under it. *(Beat.)* I ain't mad you didn't come down to Stringtown to meet me when I got out, but you might at leasta been ready for me back here. Shit, it don't even look like you knew I was comin'.

AGNES.   I didn't.

GOSS.   I wrote you a letter. Didn't you get my letter?

AGNES.   No.

GOSS.   Huh. *(Beat.)* You look good. You lost weight.

AGNES.   Not really.

GOSS.   Yeah, you did. You got somethin' sweet around here? Some Oreos or somethin'? I got a sweet tooth. *(She doesn't respond.)* Hey. Oreos?

AGNES.   No …

GOSS.   Graham cracker maybe? *(Beat.)* I was gonna getcha some flowers.

AGNES.   Jerry. Get out.

GOSS.   I just got here. I got some business to clear up down in Healdton, take me a week or two, then I'll be back up. I don't have a lot of stuff, so don't rearrange the furniture or nothin'. *(During the above, Agnes climbs out of bed to put on her clothes. Goss has his back to her, but catches her by the end of the speech.)*

AGNES.   Goss …

GOSS.   You ain't seen Mickey, have you? I hear he's lookin' for me.

AGNES. He got his parole, too?

GOSS. He did his time.

AGNES. He's an egg-suckin' son of a bitch.

GOSS. He may turn up here.

AGNES. No, he won't.

GOSS. Aw, now ... you two was always kinda sweet on each other. You didn't think I noticed, but I saw what was goin' on. Little looks, 'n all that. Little touches.

AGNES. Is that why you ratted him out?

GOSS. Yeah. *(Goss licks his finger, traces it through the coke dust on the table, runs it over his gums.)* You still snortin' this stuff?

AGNES. Apparently.

GOSS. No wonder you got so skinny.

AGNES. I didn't get skinny, you just got fatter ...

GOSS. You crack me up. You still workin' over to that honky-tonk?

AGNES. You know I am.

GOSS. Still runnin' with that li'l queer gal?

AGNES. R.C.

GOSS. You ain't gone queer on me, have you?

AGNES. You better believe it.

GOSS. You know what I'd do if I really thought that.

AGNES. Don't threaten me. I'd get another court order if I thought it'd do any —

GOSS. You shouldn'ta done that.

AGNES. You broke my door in.

GOSS. You wouldn't open it.

AGNES. I don't have to open it, Jerry.

GOSS. Aggie. I ain't interested in all this history. I got bigger fish to fry.

AGNES. You tried to kill me.

GOSS. Well ... that was a rough one. I was bad to drink back then.

AGNES. You mean back before you found God.

GOSS. Who was that boy over here last night?

AGNES. You been watchin' my place.

GOSS. I seen him leave.

AGNES. Callin' me eight times a day.

GOSS. I ain't called you once.

AGNES. Right —

GOSS. Who was he?

AGNES. He's nobody.

GOSS. Why's he comin' outta here at ten in the mornin'?

AGNES. He musta spent the night.

GOSS. Yeah, he must have.

AGNES. I do somethin' wrong?

GOSS. I don't know. Did you?

AGNES. You're ridiculous —

GOSS. You do somethin' wrong, Aggie?

AGNES. Don't do this, Goss —

GOSS. I'm not doin' nothin'.

AGNES. I just don't wanna start this all over again —

GOSS. I didn't start nothin'. I didn't know better, I'd think you ain't happy to see me. I missed you somethin' awful. Didn't you miss me?

AGNES. I can't say I did, no.

GOSS. That hurts. Sittin' there, two years, waitin' for this.

AGNES. Don't gimme that —

GOSS. God's truth. Waitin' for this. Here. You. *(He makes a move to embrace her and she pulls away.)* What's the matter, you shy? We'll get over that.

AGNES. I swear to God … y'know, I don't know if you're serious with this shit, or what … I hate you, Jerry. I wish like Christ I'd taken Lloyd out to San Diego — *(He slaps her and she goes down.)*

GOSS. I was in a good mood when I come here. Looked forward to seein' you again. But you know not to mention his name to me. I ain't the one who lost him. Now whose fault is it you just got slugged?

AGNES. Mine.

GOSS. You got some time to get your ducks in a line before I get back here. Maybe next time I come home, you can try bein' a little nicer to me. We can have a civilized conversation. Y'hear me talkin' to you?

AGNES. Yeah.

GOSS. You just remember … *(Key in the door. Peter enters, carrying a sack of muffins.)* Hidy.

PETER. Hello. *(Goss extends his hand and Peter shakes it.)*

GOSS. Jerry Goss.

PETER. Hi. *(Peter sees Agnes on the floor. He starts to go to her, but Goss blocks his path, keeps shaking hands.)*

AGNES. Goss —

GOSS. *(To Peter.)* Didn't catch the name.

PETER. Peter.

GOSS. Peter. Just … "Peter"?

PETER. Peter Evans.

GOSS. "Peter Evanth." Okay. *(Lets go of his hand.)* Aggie, where's your purse? *(Agnes points to her purse. Goss grabs money, suitcase, heads for the door.)* I love you, Aggie. See you real soon. *(He leaves. Peter goes to Agnes, helps her to the bed.)*

AGNES. Jesus, what a punch.

PETER. Are you okay?

AGNES. He's a big old boy.

PETER. Do you need anything? Let me get you a rag, or —

AGNES. Grab me some aspirins, would you? *(Peter exits to the bathroom, reenters with a wet washcloth and a bottle of aspirin, gives them to Agnes, takes the bottle back from her.)*

PETER. Can I have a couple, for my tooth?

AGNES. Sure. *(Beat.)* Thanks. Thank you for helping me.

PETER. I didn't really do anything.

AGNES. Where'd you go? I woke up —

PETER. I went out to get us some food. I hope you don't mind I took the key.

AGNES. No, that's okay. *(Peter takes two frosted muffins out of the sack, places them on the bed. Agnes chooses one, Peter takes the other, and they eat.)*

PETER. Who was that guy?

AGNES. My ex-husband. He's a nut.

PETER. Maybe you should think about some kind of security.

AGNES. Like an attack dog. Could you make me a vodka and Coke?

PETER. Yes.

AGNES. You can fire up that pipe if you want, I don't have to work tonight.

PETER. Okay.

AGNES. *(Tilting her head back.)* Any more blood?

PETER. No. *(She tosses the washcloth into the bathroom while Peter fixes the freebase pipe. During the following, they share hits on the pipe.)* How long were you married?

AGNES. Long enough to still get scared at night.

PETER. Do you have any kids?

AGNES. No.

PETER. I don't like that guy. I don't like that he hit you.

AGNES. I ain't crazy about it my own self.

PETER. He said he's coming back here.

AGNES. Eventually.

PETER. Maybe you need a gun.

AGNES. I can take care of myself.

PETER. Then why do you get scared at night?

AGNES. I's just kiddin'.

PETER. You should be scared.

AGNES. How's that?

PETER. People can do things to you, things you don't even know about.

AGNES. What kind of things?

PETER. They try to control you. They try to force you to act a certain way. They can drive you crazy, too. *(The air conditioner cuts off.)* I shouldn't talk about it. I don't know if it's safe or not.

AGNES. I think we're safe.

PETER. No, not really. You're never really safe. One time, maybe, a long time ago, people were safe, but that's all over. Not any more, not on this planet. We'll never really be safe again. We can't be, not with all the technology, and the chemicals, and the information.

AGNES. I don't even like to think about it.

PETER. Sometimes, though, when you're lying in bed at night, you can feel it. All the machines, people working their machines, their works, humming. I don't like to go on about it, 'cause it freaks people out. It freaks me out. I wish I didn't think about it, either, but they don't let you forget. They want you to know they're there.

AGNES. What's there, the ... machines?

PETER. Nothing makes them happier than knowing that people are aware the machines are up and running.

AGNES. That's some pretty wild shit.

PETER. Yeah, I know you hate me. *(Freeze. A helicopter buzzes distantly, very faintly.)*

AGNES. Why would I hate you?

PETER. I don't know.

AGNES. I don't hate you.

PETER. Okay.

AGNES. You think I hate you?

PETER. I don't know.

AGNES. I wouldn't ask you to stay here if I hated you.

PETER. I guess that's right. Unless ... I guess that's right.

AGNES. You helped me just now. We're friends.

PETER. We are?

AGNES. Sure we are. I don't have a lot of friends, but the ones I do have, I'm good to.

PETER. But you don't trust me.

AGNES. Why do you say that?

PETER. Because you lied to me about having children.

AGNES. How do you know that?

PETER. I told you, I pick up on stuff.

AGNES. I didn't lie to you. I don't have any children. I did. I did have a child, once.

PETER. What happened?

AGNES. I lost him.

PETER. He died?

AGNES. No, he disappeared.

PETER. Really?

AGNES. Yes. In a grocery store. Nine years ago. Almost ten years ago.

PETER. How old was he?

AGNES. Six.

PETER. I'm sorry.

AGNES. Got any other questions?

PETER. No.

AGNES. Ask me now, if you do. 'Cause I don't want to talk about it again.

PETER. What was his name?

AGNES. Lloyd.

PETER. When did you stop looking for him?

AGNES. Coupla years ago. Except for when I sleep. I still look for him in my sleep.

PETER. Do you ever — ?

AGNES. No. *(Beat.)* I did lie to you, about one thing. I really do get scared at night. You can stay here again, if you want.

PETER. All right.

AGNES. I kinda liked havin' someone else here for a change. Kinda nice.

PETER. I haven't been to bed with a woman for a long time, but I think I could go to bed with you. *(She stares at him, then begins to cry. He stands still, watching her. Finally, she wipes her tears, downs the rest of her vodka, stubs out her cigarette, faces him, and extends her hand.)*

AGNES. C'mere, boy … *(Blackout. In the blackout, helicopter fades away. Traffic dies …)*

Scene 3

In darkness.

PETER. Motherfucker. *(Long pause.)* Motherfucker. *(Long pause.)* You little — *(Long pause.)* Come here, you … *(Beat.)* Fucking … motherfucker. *(Beat.)* Fuck. Fuck, FUCK! FUCK IT, MAN! *(Agnes wakes, turns on a bedside lamp. Peter is scratching his wrist.)*
AGNES. What's the matter? Is it — ?
PETER. Fucking shit —
AGNES. Is it your tooth?
PETER. Fucking bug, a fucking bug bite, fuck this —
AGNES. A bug? *(Peter snaps on his bedside table light.)*
PETER. Where are you, you little motherfucker?
AGNES. What kind of bug — ?
PETER. Look at these bites. *(He shows her his wrist.)*
AGNES. Jesus, those look like spider bites —
PETER. No, I felt it a second ago, it's like a bedbug or some shit.
AGNES. Maybe you killed it.
PETER. No, I had it between my fingers, but it squiggled out.
AGNES. Pull back the covers. *(On his knees, still in bed, Peter pulls back the covers.)* I don't see it.
PETER. Little fucker, I was just about to fall asleep. *(Agnes gets out of bed, turns on the bathroom light.)*
AGNES. I don't see it —
PETER. There.
AGNES. What.
PETER. Right there.
AGNES. Where.
PETER. There.
AGNES. Where?
PETER. There, you see it?
AGNES. What.
PETER. The bug.
AGNES. Where.
PETER. Right there.
AGNES. I don't …

PETER. Right. There.

AGNES. This?

PETER. No. This. That. There.

AGNES. Where?

PETER. There! Right there, Agnes, it's right there!

AGNES. Hey, don't get all —

PETER. Well, do you see it?

AGNES. I'm not sure.

PETER. Right there. It's really small.

AGNES. I … I guess … what is that?

PETER. It's a fucking bug.

AGNES. No, I know, what kind of bug?

PETER. Like an aphid.

AGNES. A what?

PETER. An aphid, it's like a, a, a —

AGNES. A bedbug?

PETER. No, well, yeah, kind of, more like a louse.

AGNES. A louse? Like lice?

PETER. Not like head lice. They're more like plant lice.

AGNES. Like a termite.

PETER. No, that's more like a thrip.

AGNES. What's a thrip?

PETER. It's like a termite.

AGNES. Do you mean ticks?

PETER. No, a tick's like a flea, a thrip's like a termite.

AGNES. What's a bedbug like?

PETER. A bedbug.

AGNES. But what *is* a bedbug?

PETER. A bedbug.

AGNES. I thought it was just a nickname.

PETER. This is an aphid.

AGNES. Plant lice?

PETER. I think so.

AGNES. And they bite?

PETER. That one sure did.

AGNES. Then maybe it's not an orchid, or whatever —

PETER. Aphid.

AGNES. Aphid, schmafid, fuckin' kill it already, 'n let's get some sleep. *(Peter pinches the bug between his fingers.)*

PETER.	AGNES.
Little fucker.	That showed him …

(Agnes flops back down on the bed.)
PETER. Hold on. Get up.
AGNES. How come?
PETER. There might be more.
AGNES. There's not any more. We would've seen 'em.
PETER. You almost didn't see that one.
AGNES. Well, it's small.
PETER. That's my point, Agnes, they're small. We might not have seen them. *(Agnes gets up, lights a cigarette, fixes the freebase pipe. Peter strips the blanket and sheets from the mattress. During the following, they take turns hitting the pipe.)*
AGNES. Oh, Jesus Christ, if I knew —
PETER. Look at my wrist. Do you want to wake up in the morning and find this?
AGNES. I am awake, and it is the morning. *(Peter inspects the mattress, closely.)* They travel in packs or something?
PETER. Packs?
AGNES. You got reason to suspect if you find one there's others with him?
PETER. Makes sense. And you're assuming it's a him, some rogue aphid on his travels, instead of some matriarchal type with a big brood somewhere.
AGNES. What's matriarchal?
PETER. Did you ever watch *Big Valley?*
AGNES. Sure.
PETER. Barbara Stanwyck?
AGNES. Yeah.
PETER. Like her.
AGNES. Oh …
PETER. This is clean. Give me the fitted sheet. *(She hands him the sheet and he inspects it.)*
AGNES. You want a drink?
PETER. Do you?
AGNES. Might as well.
PETER. You drink a lot.
AGNES. Fuck off.
PETER. I didn't mean it in a … pejorative sense. *(She shoots him the finger, raspberry included.)* I drink a lot, too.
AGNES. So maybe you shoulda said, "*We* drink a lot," in a pejorative sense.
PETER. Okay. We drink a lot.

25

AGNES. You want one?

PETER. Sure.

AGNES. Where'd you learn to talk like that, anyway?

PETER. From books.

AGNES. In school.

PETER. I didn't go to school.

AGNES. College.

PETER. School. I was home-schooled.

AGNES. No shit.

PETER. My father didn't believe in school.

AGNES. He musta done a good job, throwin' around words like "matriarchal."

PETER. Well, I learned that from *Big Valley*. Here, this's clean. Give me the top sheet. *(He throws the fitted sheet onto the bed and takes the top sheet from her to continue his inspection. The air conditioner comes on.)*

AGNES. You got a nice body.

PETER. So do you.

AGNES. It's better lookin' without clothes on.

PETER. I agree.

AGNES. You know how some folks look nice with clothes on, but you get 'em naked, they're a big disappointment.

PETER. Yeah.

AGNES. Why'd you say you weren't much for the ladies?

PETER. It's true.

AGNES. Coulda fooled me.

PETER. You're different.

AGNES. How am I different?

PETER. You don't speak the codes.

AGNES. How long's it been since you was with a woman?

PETER. I don't know. A few years.

AGNES. You musta got a bad one.

PETER. I just decided it wasn't worth it any more.

AGNES. What wasn't? I mean, how do you mean — ?

PETER. You have a center, right? I mean, a place, inside, that's just you, that hasn't been spoiled. I think it's important to try to keep that place sacred, in some sense, on some level, but sex, or relationships, they cloud that space. Or, they cloud me, I guess, and make it difficult to be just me, and not to have to worry about being someone else. I sound like some big asshole, don't I?

AGNES. No. I like to hear you talk. *(She touches him, maybe even embraces him. He turns away.)*

PETER. Hand me the blanket. *(He tosses the top sheet back on the bed and she gives him the blanket.)*

AGNES. You musta missed gettin' laid.

PETER. Not really. You have a lot of energy in your seed. Not you, one does. A man does.

AGNES. Don't you even jack off?

PETER. Huh-uh.

AGNES. Jesus … *(The phone rings. Once, twice.)*

PETER. Aren't you going to answer it?

AGNES. Huh-uh.

PETER. Why not?

AGNES. It's Goss.

PETER. You were Goss once. *(She doesn't respond. Peter answers the phone, drops his voice.)* Hello? *(Beat.)* Hello? *(Peter jerks the phone away from his ear and hangs up.)*

AGNES. Goss.

PETER. I don't think so.

AGNES. What'd they say?

PETER. Just static. *(Peter resumes his inspection of the mattress, spots another bug.)* There you go. See?

AGNES. Where?

PETER. There.

AGNES. I'm sorry, where again?

PETER. Right there.

AGNES. Squish him.

PETER. There you go again. How do you know it's not the super-mother aphid, and she's carrying a million eggs?

AGNES. What the hell are plant lice doin' in my place?

PETER. *(Whilst squishing.)* Biting me, for one thing.

AGNES. I have to get the place sprayed.

PETER. I'll do it. I'll buy some stuff tomorrow.

AGNES. Fuck that, it's their room, they should spray it.

PETER. But someone will have to come in here.

AGNES. Damn right.

PETER. Well … you do what you want, but I wouldn't …

AGNES. How come?

PETER. Hand me the pillows. *(He tosses the blanket back on the bed and she gives him the pillows. He strips the pillowcases.)*

AGNES. How come?

PETER. Never mind.

AGNES. No, what?

PETER. No, I shouldn't have said anything.

AGNES. What?

PETER. It's your place, I don't mean to interfere —

AGNES. But why wouldn't I want someone to come in here? Goddamnit, I knew you was a con. Why didn't you tell me when — ?

PETER. I've never been to prison. I'm just ... look, I'm kind of ... I've got some people after me, that's —

AGNES. Who's after you?

PETER. It's a long story.

AGNES. If you're stayin' here, I need to know.

PETER. It's for your own benefit. I don't want to drag you into it, that's all.

AGNES. Drag me into what?

PETER. Agnes, please —

AGNES. Drag me into what?

PETER. I'm just not comfortable telling you.

AGNES. You don't trust me. I don't know you from Adam. I'm layin' here naked next to some stranger, and you don't even trust me enough —

PETER. I trust you. That's not —

AGNES. Come on, man —

PETER. I just don't want you to get hurt, can't you — ?

AGNES. I'll take my chances.

PETER. I won't. *(He tosses the pillows down, starts putting on his clothes.)*

AGNES. So you're goin'.

PETER. I should.

AGNES. Where?

PETER. I'll be fine.

AGNES. All right, then fuck off. *(He dresses silently. She puts on a robe, takes a seat on the bed.)* You may think it's easy for me to just take you in here, okay, but I ain't the kind of woman who just goes from man to man. Fact is, it's been quite awhile since I had anyone to get ... to get close to. Y'hear what I'm sayin'? Not that I need another man, I need a man like I need a hole in the head, but I just get ... I get damn lonely sometimes. It was kinda nice to have someone — *(Peter heads for the door. Agnes picks up the clock radio, heaves it at him.)* Son of a bitch! *(The radio misses him, strikes the door. She runs into the bathroom, slams the door behind her. Peter stands for a moment, listening to her sobs coming from the bathroom.*

He leaves the motel room. Empty room. The air conditioner cuts off. Silence. Twenty seconds. Peter reenters. He crosses to the bathroom, sits on the bed in front of the door. During the following, the helicopter buzzes again, gradually gets louder.)

PETER. I got in some trouble … with the Army. I was stationed at Sakaka … the Syrian Desert, during the war. The doctors came in and really worked us over, with shots and pills, ostensibly for inoculation, but … there was something else going on, too. A lot of the guys got sick, vomiting and diarrhea, migraines, blackouts. One guy had an epileptic seizure; he'd never had one before. A couple of guys went AWOL. I never found out what really happened to them. I started having weird thoughts, too, and feeling … sick. They shipped me home, put me in a hospital at Groom Lake. They started running these tests. They had every kind of doctor you could imagine, probing at me, jabbing me, asking me all kinds of weird questions, feeding me more pills. They wouldn't let me go. They kept me there — years, I don't know, four years? Those fucking doctors were experimenting on me.

I went AWOL. I was a lifer, too. I didn't have anywhere to go. They don't respond too well to some drugged-up guinea pig just taking off. I don't know that I'm not carrying some disease with me, some contagion. Jesus, you know that's how they start, typhoid, Legionnaires' disease, some government screw-up, AIDS with those fucking monkeys in Africa. They're after me. These people don't fuck around, Agnes.

I shouldn't have told you that. But I needed to tell somebody. And I do trust you. I don't think you're just some simpleton I can take advantage of. I know we haven't known each other very long, but … I like you, Agnes. I don't want to go … I don't want to go … *(The door slowly opens and Agnes comes out, wrapping herself around Peter. They hug.)*

AGNES. Don't leave me … *(She spies something in his hair, picks it out, studies it. He sees it, too. The helicopter gets even louder, approaching …)* Peter…? *(Blackout.)*

End of Act One

ACT TWO

Scene 1

Lights up on Peter. He sits cross-legged in front of a child's foot locker where he has set up his "lab": a kiddie chemistry set, with microscope, magnifying glass, petri dishes, glass slides, and vials. The weapons of a bug war surround him: cans of bug spray, from the cheap, over-the-counter items to the industrial tub with a metal spray hose; fly strips, hung from the ceiling, the lamps, the painting; roach motels, in the corner, on the table, by the fridge, under the bed; a flyswatter. On the floor, beside the bed, is a stack of assorted childhood items: crummy toys, chewed-up crayons, some clothing. The traffic continues to drone outside; a Latino couple a few doors down are having an argument, barely audible through the walls. At rise, Peter pricks his finger with an Exacto knife and squeezes a few drops of blood into a petri dish. He then carefully slides the cap from another petri dish, removes a captive bug, drops it into the petri dish that holds his blood, and quickly covers it. After giving the dish a cursory inspection with the magnifying glass, he jots a few notes in a journal, then examines the dish under the microscope. A knock on the door. Peter turns, hesitates, crosses to the door, listens. Another knock. Then, a scraping sound. Peter stares at the doorknob as it slowly turns. The door opens and Goss enters, a lock pick in his hand.

PETER. Can I help you?
GOSS. No. *(Goss closes the door, throws his hat across the room, flops on the bed, kicks his boots off.)*
PETER. Agnes isn't here.
GOSS. No shit. Where is she?
PETER. The liquor store, I think. *(Peter resumes his work at the lab. Goss slowly becomes aware of the insecticides, etc.)*
GOSS. Y'know, if I was a roach, I believe I'd take the hint. *(Peter*

30

does not respond.) Where's the TV?

PETER. I don't think she has one.

GOSS. We had one. 19-inch RCA. Sure-touch tuning. I bought it with money I made drivin' a sausage truck. I drove twenty hours a day sometimes, so I could feed my wife and my kid. You ever done anything like that? *(No response.)* Who doesn't have a TV? How're you supposed to know what's goin' on in the world? Jesus, we might get invaded by Martians or somethin'. They could be evacuatin' the whole dang city right now, 'n you and me's sittin' here with our thumbs up our butts.

PETER. Could be. *(Goss spots the child's things by the bed.)*

GOSS. Who got this stuff out?

PETER. I did. For the microscope.

GOSS. Uh-huh. *(Goss takes a little boy's shirt from the pile, unfolds it. Smells it.)* Y'little shit … *(He tosses the shirt back on the pile.)* You might want to put this stuff up before Aggie gets home. She won't like it.

PETER. Right. *(Goss sidles up next to the lab, fiddles with stuff.)*

GOSS. What'cha workin' on?

PETER. I'm — don't touch that, please — I'm just looking at something.

GOSS. What'cha lookin' at?

PETER. A bug.

GOSS. A bug.

PETER. Yes.

GOSS. "Yeth." You know who you remind me of? *(Beat.)* You know who you remind me of?

PETER. Who do I remind you of?

GOSS. Guy I knew in the pen.

PETER. In the pen.

GOSS. I just did a deuce for armed robbery.

PETER. I see —

GOSS. Anyways, I knew a guy there named Porterfield. You ain't related, are you?

PETER. I don't believe so.

GOSS. "You don't believe tho."

PETER. No.

GOSS. You know what we called him? *(Beat.)* You know what we — ?

PETER. No, what did you call him?

GOSS. Mrs. Porterfield. You kinda remind me of him.

PETER. Oh. *(Goss looks through the microscope.)*

GOSS. What the fuck am I lookin' at?

PETER. A bug. In my blood.

GOSS. In your blood.

PETER. Yes.

GOSS. "Yeth." I don't see no bug.

PETER. It's very small.

GOSS. I bet it is. You're pretty much just jackin' off here, ain'tcha? *(Beat.)* Why don't you answer me when I ask you a question?

PETER. I thought it was a rhetorical question.

GOSS. Y'know what I'd do if I thought you was fuckin' with Agnes?

PETER. Something gruesome, I imagine.

GOSS. "Thomething gruethome."

PETER. Look, I don't know who you are, and I don't know —

GOSS. You don't know who I am? Didn't we meet in here just a couple of weeks ago?

PETER. Yes —

GOSS. D'ja forget me that quick?

PETER. No.

GOSS. I remember who you are.

PETER. Right, my point is, I don't want any trouble with you —

GOSS. We ain't gonna have no trouble.

PETER. Good.

GOSS. But I'm stayin' here for a while, so you're gonna have to find somewheres else to do your li'l experiments.

PETER. I don't think you want to stay here.

GOSS. I don't. Why don't I?

PETER. The place is crawling with these things.

GOSS. With your li'l bugs?

PETER. We're infested. *(Goss takes in the room, studies Peter.)*

GOSS. I believe you are … *(The door opens and Agnes and R.C. enter.)* What'dja bring me? *(Goss gets up, hugs and kisses R.C.)*

GOSS.	AGNES.
How you been, girl?	You let him in here?
R.C.	PETER.
Been better, I suppose —	He picked the lock.

GOSS. Mustache tickles a little bit.

R.C. That's okay.

GOSS. No, I meant yours.

AGNES. You can't stay here, Goss.

GOSS. That's okay, I just need a place to hang my hat for a couple of days. *(To R.C.)* Hey, what's that gal's name you used to run with?

R.C. Lavoice.

GOSS. That's it, goddamnit, I been tryin' to think. She's a character. You remember that time she took a crap off the balcony over at Mickey's place 'n hit that police car?

R.C. Yeah —

GOSS. Lordy, I never laughed so damn hard in my goddamn life.

R.C. The pork party.

GOSS. Was that the pork party? It was, wasn't it? Hey, you remember that, Aggie?

AGNES. Jerry —

GOSS. *(Cracking up, to Peter.)* Mickey'd cooked up this big can of pork, like you get in the army. Some drunk asshole started throwin' it all over the place, and by the end of the night, there's Mickey, passed out in the corner of the kitchen … *(He becomes too tickled to talk. Weeps with laughter.)* … and he's got this big pot turned upside down on his head, pork all over his shirt … *(Cracks up even worse. He staggers into the bathroom, grabs tissue, comes back out, trailing tissue behind him.)* … he couldn't stand up 'cause the congoleum linoleum was so greasy —

AGNES. Jerry.

GOSS. I had some pictures of that —

AGNES. Get out.

GOSS. I told you, darlin', I just need a coupla weeks to —

AGNES. I want you outta here.

GOSS. Wait a second, I was just —

AGNES. Now.

GOSS. You throwin' me out?

AGNES. Yeah. I'm throwin' you out.

GOSS. Okay. *(During the following, Goss casually puts on his boots, grabs his hat.)* I just misunderstood. I thought I was gonna stay here for a while, but now I see that's a bad idea. What with you bein' infested and all. *(Beat.)* I won't lie to you, Aggie. I'm disappointed. I'd hoped for a little more from you, but I don't guess I have a right to expect that. *(Swivels to Peter.)* And I owe you an apology. I had you figured all wrong. Here I was thinkin' you're some kind of weirdo free-loadin' cokehead … but I didn't know you was takin' such good care of Aggie. Keepin' them bugs away from her … that's important. I appreciate it. *(Goss is at the door, finally.)* I'll be around. *(Goss leaves.)*

PETER. Come here and look at this.

AGNES. Jesus …

33

PETER. Come here. *(Agnes grabs the freebase pipe, hits it. R.C. goes to the phone and dials.)*

AGNES. *(To R.C.)* You believe that?

PETER. I need you to look at this now, please.

AGNES. *(To Peter, re: microscope.)* You found it.

R.C. *(To phone.)* Yeah, police department, please — *(Peter leaps to the phone, jerks it out of R.C.'s hand, slams it down.)* What the fuck —

PETER. What do you think you're doing?

R.C. I was callin' the cops.

PETER. Don't do that.

R.C. Agnes —

PETER. Don't ever do that. *(Peter returns to the microscope.)*

R.C. It's B and E, pure and simple. He violated his parole, his restrainin' order —

PETER. Agnes, will you — ?

R.C. *(To Agnes.)* Have him put away, don't mess around with him —

AGNES. It just ain't that easy.

PETER. Agnes. Please. *(Agnes goes to the microscope, looks in.)* Do you see it?

AGNES. What?

R.C. Agnes —

PETER. You see the bug?

AGNES. Yeah, I …

PETER. Can you tell what it's doing?

R.C. Agnes —

AGNES. Not really … it's so …

PETER. It's feeding.

AGNES. On what?

PETER. My blood. It's feeding off my blood.

AGNES. So … you're sayin' …

PETER. Jesus, I'm saying it's feeding off my blood. It's a parasite. *(R.C. peeks in the microscope, doesn't comment.)*

AGNES. We knew that, though.

PETER. No, we knew they were biting. Bugs bite for different reasons. These are biting for food.

R.C. *(Re: pesticides, etc.)* None of this shit's working.

PETER. They're immune to the sprays. I thought they might be coke bugs, but I couldn't find any in Agnes's stash.

R.C. What are coke bugs?

PETER. They're the bugs you sometimes find in cocaine.

R.C. Cocaine doesn't have bugs.

PETER. The DEA sprays the larvae on the coca plantations in South America, Central America. They're genetically engineered to survive the purification process. If they can't wipe out the drugs, they want to wipe out the users. You don't know about this? That's hard to believe —

AGNES. That's why you only do the rock.

PETER. Yes, it boils them away.

AGNES. Thanks for tellin' me.

PETER. They don't get to all of it. You don't have them, I told you. I checked. Believe me, if you had them …

R.C. You've had 'em before?

PETER. You ask a lot of questions.

AGNES. Maybe we should take these to a lab somewheres.

PETER. A lab. What for?

AGNES. Find out what they are.

PETER. I know what they are.

R.C. What are they?

PETER. They're blood-sucking aphids, and we're infested —

R.C. Y'know, this aphid business —

AGNES. *(To Peter.)* What is this? *(Agnes shows Peter her elbow. R.C. gets a closer look, too.)*

PETER. It's a burrowing aphid. You have to dig it out.

R.C. Lemme see … *(Peter grabs a safety pin and hands it to Agnes as R.C. studies her elbow.)* Where is it?

AGNES.   PETER.
It's right there.   On her elbow.

R.C. Where?

AGNES. You see it? That speck?

R.C. I can't see shit.

AGNES. Look, just under the skin.

R.C.   PETER.
I don't see shit.   It's there.

R.C. Why can't I see it?

AGNES.   PETER.
It's real itty-bitty, you   I don't know why. Why
really gotta look for it.   can we see it?

R.C. It's under the skin?

AGNES. Yeah. Here, I'll dig it out, you can see it better.

PETER. The place is crawling with them. *(Agnes digs at her elbow with the needle.)*

AGNES. Y'know, when I talked to Carl, he said nobody else has even —

PETER. Wait a minute, wait a minute. You talked to who?

AGNES. Carl, the manager. Of the motel.

PETER. Why? Whose idea — ?

AGNES. To tell him we were infested with —

PETER. Why'd you tell him that?

R.C. Why shouldn't she?

PETER. Tell me what you told him. Tell me exactly.

AGNES. I didn't tell him anything that'd get you into any —

PETER. We agreed we weren't going to tell —

AGNES. We're the only ones who've even seen 'em —

R.C. *(Raising hand.)* I haven't seen 'em —

AGNES. Don't you think that's a little weird? We got people all around us —

PETER. So what are you saying?

AGNES. I'm saying … it's a little weird —

PETER. You already said that —

R.C. We saw a doctor.

AGNES. Ronnie …

R.C. She had to know about those sores.

PETER. *(To Agnes.)* Either you don't really grasp the situation here, or you're just fucking me over —

AGNES. I didn't mention you. I didn't mention anything about —

PETER. What kind of doctor?

AGNES. A dermatologist.

PETER. And what did he find?

R.C. No bugs.

PETER. *(To Agnes.)* You picked them off.

R.C. He said they didn't even look like bug bites.

PETER. *(To R.C.)* Excuse me. Will you please not talk while I address Agnes?

AGNES. He gave me some stuff for a rash —

PETER. Let me see it. *(He finds her purse, pulls out a tube of prescription ointment.)*

AGNES. It's just a lotion — *(He throws the tube into the bathroom.)*

PETER. They got to you. Goddamnit, if you're a part of this —

AGNES. Maybe we've been hittin' the pipe too heavy —

PETER. This is not a hallucinogen. *(To R.C.)* Tell her this is not a hallucinogen —

AGNES. I'm just lookin' for some kind of explanation —

PETER. You tell me: Do we have bugs or not?

AGNES. I think so.

PETER. It's not a matter of opinion. An organism just *is,* or it *isn't.*

AGNES. Right.

PETER. So … *are* the bugs, or *aren't* they?

AGNES. *Some* are, I know —

PETER. No, not *some* bugs. Don't give me *some* bugs. *Presence* of bugs, *absence* of bugs. The sign outside says, "Vacancies," or "No Vacancies." It doesn't say, *"Possibility* of Vacancies," that's understood. Now, do we have bugs or not?

AGNES. Yeah.

PETER. Then your *doctor* is *lying* to you.

R.C. Peter. Do you have bites like hers?

AGNES. Worse than me. Show her. *(Peter pulls up his shirt. His chest and stomach are covered with sores and scratches. The sores on his stomach are arranged in a large circular pattern. One sore, quite infected, maybe two inches in diameter, marks the center of the circle.)*

R.C. Oh, my God …

AGNES. Did you put somethin' on that — ?

R.C. And you believe an *aphid* did that to you?

PETER. I know what did it to me.

R.C. Aphids can't bite.

PETER. Do you know a lot about aphids?

R.C. No.

PETER. Do you know anything about aphids?

R.C. No.

PETER. We do. *(Peter and R.C. are now locked onto each other.)*

AGNES. C'mon, y'all, let's, Ronnie, tell him your news. *(To Peter.)* Lavoice got custody of her kid. Ain't that great news? Ronnie's gonna be a mother, or an aunt or whatever.

PETER. That's terrific.

AGNES. I just can't believe it, not in Oklahoma.

R.C. Y'all listen to me now. There ain't no bugs.

AGNES. C'mon —

R.C. There ain't no bugs in the microscope, on your skin, *in* your skin. In the room. *There ain't no fuckin' bugs.*

PETER. That's odd that you —

R.C. Peter, I was there, with the doctor. Tell him what he told you, Agnes.

AGNES. I don't think we should —

R.C. He said her sores were "self-inflicted." She's done this to herself, just like you. Or you done it to her.

37

PETER. You think I —

R.C. I don't know what your deal is. I don't know who you are, or what you're all about, and I don't give a damn, but I by God regret the day I brought you over here.

AGNES. Ronnie —

R.C. I can't do nothin' about you, except suggest you get some serious medical attention, but I can do somethin' about my friend, and I by God intend to.

PETER. Do you? What do you — ?

R.C. Yeah, I'm takin' her outta here, and she'll come stay with me for a while.

AGNES. Ronnie, I can't —

R.C. Try and stop me. I'll reintroduce you to an old friend of yours.

PETER. What does that mean?

R.C. Somebody's been askin' about you.

AGNES. Who?

PETER. Somebody asking about —

R.C. Dr. Sweet.

AGNES. Who's Dr. Sweet? What are you talkin' about?

PETER. Think about it. Think about what your friend is doing.

R.C. You know what I'm talkin' about.

PETER. Yes, I do. *(To Agnes.)* Groom Lake. Your friend is going to turn me in.

AGNES. Tell me —

R.C. He come into the bar, askin' about Peter.

PETER. What did he tell you?

R.C. Not much. I didn't even know you were stayin' here, so I guess I didn't ask enough questions. But he's nobody you wanna see, or he'da known how to find you.

AGNES. Don't play games with him now —

R.C. I ain't playin'.

PETER. No. You're not.

AGNES. It's okay, she's not gonna do that —

R.C. Try me.

AGNES. Ronnie, stop it, you don't mean it —

R.C. Try me.

PETER. I'm … stunned … that you think I would try to stop Agnes from going with you. I'm only staying here because I was invited. I don't stay where I'm not wanted, and I certainly wouldn't attempt to keep somebody where they don't want to be. Agnes is an adult. She's free to do as she pleases.

R.C. I thought you might see it that way.

PETER. As for Dr. Sweet, tell him what you wish. I have no doubt he already knows where I am.

R.C. Right.

PETER. But as for your contention that there are no bugs … I disagree. *(The air conditioner comes on.)*

R.C. *(To Agnes.)* You wanna pack a bag, come stay with me for awhile? *(Peter suddenly slaps his neck, brushes at his hair. He staggers backward, slapping at his arms, his face, his hair, his neck, the air in front of him.)*

AGNES.	R.C.
Peter, what's — ?	Jesus Christ —

PETER. Motherfuckers — *(His slapping and brushing become frantic, panicked. He grabs a coat hanger, beats himself with it, spinning in a circle, screaming:)* MOTHERFUCKERS! GET OFF ME, MOTHER-FUCKERS! *(Agnes and R.C. jump to their feet, uncertain, wanting to help. Peter goes into a frenzy, scratching, slapping, shrieking.)*

AGNES.	R.C.
Peter! Peter!	Oh my God — !

(They move toward him. He jumps away.)

PETER. DON'T PUT THEM ON ME DON'T PUT THEM ON ME WHY ARE YOU DOING THIS WHY ARE YOU DOING THIS!

AGNES.	R.C.
How can we help you?!	I'm not doing anything,
What do we do?!	I'm just — !

(He jumps into the corner of the room, spins madly in a circle, hammering his body against the walls.)

AGNES. Peter, God, stop! *(Agnes grabs the blanket, rushes him, wraps the blanket around him, pulls him to the floor. He writhes wildly underneath the blanket and now appears to be having an epileptic seizure. Agnes and R.C. hold onto him until the seizure ends and he lays silent, apparently passed out. Agnes suddenly lashes out, pushes R.C. away.)* Who do you think you are? You come in here and try to take away the only thing in the world I have, that's mine. Why can't I have one thing? Why can't you leave me with one thing? Get out. Get out of here, and don't ever come back. *(R.C. exits. Agnes hugs Peter, rocks him, soothes him. Blackout. In the blackout: The air conditioner cuts off. Buzz of the helicopter.)*

Scene 2

Note: From this point on, Agnes and Peter often kill bugs, swat them away from their faces, etc. Lights up on Agnes and Peter laying in bed. Peter groans, softly at first, then louder.

AGNES. Is it your tooth?

PETER. Yes ... oohhhh, Christ ...

AGNES. You have to go to a dentist.

PETER. I already had it filled — I don't understand ...

AGNES. Take some more aspirin.

PETER. I finished them.

AGNES. You finished the whole bottle? Today?

PETER. Yes ...

AGNES. I might have a codeine in there ... *(A long silence.)* Peter?

PETER. Yes.

AGNES. Let's leave. I can't take it any more.

PETER. We can't. They're watching.

AGNES. Seems like if they knew where you were, they'd just grab you.

PETER. They're playing with me.

AGNES. Can't we sneak out?

PETER. It's too risky. *(Another silence.)*

AGNES. I have a sister in San Diego. She'd take us in 'til we got on our feet. *(Beat.)* I was gonna take Lloyd out there ... get away from Goss. She invited us. But I waited too long. Who knows, maybe she hates me now, too. *(Beat.)* I can't believe R.C. did that to me. I can't imagine what I did to her to make her hate me so much. I don't know why I couldn't see it before. Spyin' little bitch. *(Beat.)* I don't know why I love you so much. I don't even know you very well. We ain't really done much in bed, except for that one night, and for some reason, I don't even care. Seems like all we ever talk about is bugs. I guess I'd rather talk about bugs with you than talk about nothin' with nobody. Not like I really got a lot to say, 'less I talk about misery, but who wants to hear that all the time? I don't. I just get sick of it, my lousy life, laundromats and grocery stores, dumb marriages and lost kids. Lloyd ... he's the only good time. *(Beat.)*

40

I'm forty-four. *(Peter snaps on the bedside lamp, sits upright in bed.)*
PETER. That's it.
AGNES. What?
PETER. I get it now.
AGNES. Tell me.
PETER. We're the only ones. No one else in the motel has bugs.
AGNES. Yeah.
PETER. Because they're my bugs. I brought them here. They came from me. *(Peter gets out of bed, stalks the room. During the following, Agnes fixes the freebase pipe, hits it.)*
AGNES. What makes you think that?
PETER. You didn't have them before I came.
AGNES. You're sayin' they were in your clothes, or what?
PETER. My skin. They're in my skin. Under my skin.
AGNES. How's that?
PETER. There's an egg sac under my skin.
AGNES. Egg sac.
PETER. That's why they didn't grab me.
AGNES. But I thought they're suckin' your blood or whatever, so why would —
PETER. I'm not a biologist, all right? The eggs are under my skin, they hatch, they need air, they come out, they need food, they come back, they eat.
AGNES. So how'd the eggs get in there to start with?
PETER. Think about it. *(Peter rummages roughly through the top shelf of Agnes's closet.)*
AGNES. They wouldn'ta done that to you.
PETER. Who would they have done it to, a pig? They have to try it on a human, see if it works before they start spraying Baghdad with insect eggs. *(He knocks a plastic toolbox to the floor, rummages through its spilled contents.)*
AGNES. But you're an American, a U.S. soldier —
PETER. Oh, right, what was I thinking? Our government wouldn't conduct experiments on their own people —
AGNES. No.
PETER. — like feeding LSD to enlisted men at Edgewood Arsenal, or, or, or sitting around watching those poor fuckers in Tuskegee die from syphilis. Why don't you fucking wake up — ?
AGNES. So where is this egg sac? *(Peter turns up a pair of pliers, places them in his mouth, over a tooth.)* What are you — ? *(He clamps the pliers, hard, and pulls, crying out.)* Peter! Stop it! *(He drops the*

41

pliers, paces, hand over his mouth. The phone rings, maybe a dozen times, unanswered.) What the fuck are you doin'?!

PETER. The sac is in my tooth.

AGNES. You can't put an egg sac in your tooth.

PETER. I had it filled at the base. Sadistic sons-of-bitches put an insect egg sac under the filling —

AGNES. Maybe we just got a little bug problem here —

PETER. They're eating me!

AGNES. I know, I know, I'm just playin' devil's advocate here —

PETER. All right —

AGNES. Maybe you're just lookin' for a connection to the army —

PETER. No, bullshit —

AGNES. — so you're more liable to see one —

PETER. — bullshit, bullshit —

AGNES. Just bear with me —

PETER. You don't know what you're talking about. You have no idea what these people are capable of. *(She puts her hand to his cheek —)*

AGNES. Peter — *(— and he slaps it away sharply.)*

PETER. I am not a child. I know who I am. *(He picks up the pliers, walks to the bathroom, looks in the mirror.)*

AGNES. Let's at least go to a real dentist —

PETER. It's just not safe. I'm being watched too closely —

AGNES. You can't know that.

PETER. They haven't grabbed me because they want to see how the experiment turns out —

AGNES. Peter, stop it! Give me those! *(She attempts to get the pliers away from him. He pushes her away, not violently, but firmly. Again, he places the pliers over the molar. Counts to three silently —)* Peter, stop it! Don't! *(— then clamps and pulls. Hard. He screams.)* Stop it! *(He relaxes for a moment, and now, with renewed force, clamps hard, pulls, pulls, sweating, screaming —)* STOP IT! *(— and yanks the molar out of his mouth.)* Oh, God — *(Blood streams freely from his mouth, onto his chest, onto the sink, onto the floor …)* I'm gonna be sick … *(Peter carries the tooth to the microscope, pinches it in the pliers until it breaks apart. He taps the tooth fragments into a petri dish, looks at the petri dish through the microscope. He backs away from the microscope, giggling, pointing at the evidence. Agnes goes to the microscope and looks in …)* Millions … *(Blackout. In the blackout: knocking on the door.)*

Scene 3

Lights up on the dark, empty room. The walls and windows have been papered with tinfoil; rolls of unused tinfoil and a staple gun sit by the door. A stool covered with a bedsheet sits in front of the table. Knocking on the door continues.

DR. SWEET. *(Offstage.)* Is this the White residence? *(A long silence.)* I'm looking for Peter Evans. I was told I could find him here. *(Beat.)* Ms. White? *(Beat.)* I have it on good authority that Peter is staying here. *(Beat.)* I don't mean any harm. If I could just talk to Peter … *(Beat.)* Could I speak with you for a moment? *(Beat.)* I assure you, I'm here with the best of intentions. *(Beat.)* All right. Thank you. *(The bathroom door opens a crack. Agnes peeks out, looks around the room, tiptoes to the front door. She puts her ear against the door, then looks through the peephole. She creeps to the window, pulls the shade back, tries to see outside. She stares at the door, backs away. The door explodes open, and Goss enters, followed by Dr. Sweet. Agnes goes for Goss, but he pins her arms.)*

AGNES. Dirty mother —

GOSS. Settle down — ! *(Goss throws her on the bed.)*

AGNES. You ain't takin' me! *(Dr. Sweet takes a billfold out of his suit jacket, tosses it to her.)*

DR. SWEET. I'm Phillip Sweet. All of my credentials are in there.

AGNES. As if you couldn't fake that!

GOSS. Just listen to the man.

AGNES. You're in way over your head, Jerry.

DR. SWEET. *(To Goss.)* Why don't you wait outside? Give us some time alone. *(Goss hesitates, leaves. Dr. Sweet stares at Agnes, then surveys the room.)* Bug problem?

AGNES. You should know.

DR. SWEET. I should? *(Beat.)* What are they?

AGNES. Aphids.

DR. SWEET. Aphids.

AGNES. Look around you, asshole. *(He gives the room a cursory glance.)* They're *in* right now. They go in when they feel like it.

DR. SWEET. And the tinfoil…?

43

AGNES. Scrambles the signal.

DR. SWEET. You're receiving a signal.

AGNES. Transmitting.

DR. SWEET. You're transmitting a signal.

AGNES. Not me. The bugs.

DR. SWEET. The bugs have a transmitter.

AGNES. They are transmitters.

DR. SWEET. And the tinfoil scrambles the signal.

AGNES. It helps.

DR. SWEET. I'm sure it does. *(Beat.)* Peter Evans has been incarcerated in an army hospital for four years.

AGNES. I know.

DR. SWEET. He's been diagnosed as a delusional paranoid with schizophrenic tendencies, although personally, I'm not a big fan of labels. His doctors believe he's potentially dangerous to himself, or even others.

AGNES. Aren't you his doctor?

DR. SWEET. More of a consultant, really.

AGNES. He told me about you. He says you got a kick out of it, like some Nazi.

DR. SWEET. Got a kick out of it …

AGNES. Your experiments.

DR. SWEET. My experiments. So now he's being hunted by the Army, the CIA … and you think they'd send a doctor to find him. *(Beat.)* I'm here on my own.

AGNES. 'Cause you care about Peter so much.

DR. SWEET. Yes, I do.

AGNES. Uh-huh.

DR. SWEET. Know why he was institutionalized?

AGNES. No.

DR. SWEET. No, you wouldn't. May I have a drink?

AGNES. No, you can't.

DR. SWEET. *(Gestures to pipe.)* How often do you hit that thing?

AGNES. As often as I feel like.

DR. SWEET. May I? *(Dr. Sweet takes a seat on the covered stool, fixes the pipe. Agnes watches as he strikes the lighter.)*

AGNES. I'd be careful lightin' that up.

DR. SWEET. I'm okay.

AGNES. You're also sittin' on ten gallons of hi-test. *(He pulls back the bedsheet, revealing two five-gallon jerry cans.)*

DR. SWEET. I can only guess what this is for. I don't see a jet ski in here. *(He hits the pipe.)* Bugs are a fairly common delusion among paranoids. Bugs, spiders, snakes, spiders. You haven't had any snakes, have you?

AGNES. You're the first.

DR. SWEET. Have you at least entertained the idea that the bugs are a delusion?

AGNES. How do I know you're not a delusion?

DR. SWEET. Touché. *(She jerks her head back, smacks her hands in front of her. She shows a smashed bug to Dr. Sweet. He studies it, looks at her.)* Well … that's no delusion. Where do the bugs come from?

AGNES. Peter.

DR. SWEET. How does that work?

AGNES. You injected him.

DR. SWEET. I injected him. Right. When did *you* first see the bugs?

AGNES. When they got here.

DR. SWEET. He saw them first.

AGNES. They're his bugs.

DR. SWEET. Yes, they are. And when I take him away, they'll disappear. *(Beat.)* You want the bugs to disappear.

AGNES. I can handle it. We're winnin' the fight.

DR. SWEET. Really. The bugs are … retreating.

AGNES. No. But now we can find the egg sacs on his body and cut them out.

DR. SWEET. You keep up that cutting, and there might not be much of Peter left. For you or for me.

AGNES. I know what I'm doing. *(The helicopter buzzes faintly. Sweet watches Agnes react to the sound. He crosses to the radio, turns it on, a little too loud.)*

DR. SWEET. You're being watched. *(Beat.)* I could talk to them. They'd listen to me.

AGNES. Yeah…?

DR. SWEET. Oh, yes. I'm very big. I'm very important. Peter comes in out of the cold, first thing I'll do is get him in surgery so they can cut out those eggs.

AGNES. Egg sacs.

DR. SWEET. Egg sacs. Simple procedure, under the proper conditions, with a trained medical staff.

AGNES. They'll put him back in the hospital. They'll take him away from me.

DR. SWEET. No, they won't. I won't let them.

AGNES. Can you do that?

45

DR. SWEET. I am his doctor. He is my project.

AGNES. He is.

DR. SWEET. I don't want him locked up. I want to help him.

AGNES. Why? Why would you stop what you started?

DR. SWEET. We made a mistake. I made a mistake. I didn't realize … I didn't know what they were using it for. What they're doing … it's dangerous. It's wrong. *(Sweet takes a notepad from his pocket, scribbles a number on it, gives it to Agnes.)* Have him call me. Let me take him in. Because if you leave it in their hands, I can't vouch for Peter's chances.

AGNES. Why are they doing this?

DR. SWEET. It's what they do.

AGNES. I can't trust you.

DR. SWEET. Yes, you can. I can do something for you. I can help you. *(Beat.)* Your son. Lloyd.

AGNES. What do you know about Lloyd? How do you — ?

DR. SWEET. I know about Lloyd. I can help you find Lloyd.

AGNES. You know about —

DR. SWEET. I shouldn't say anything more.

AGNES. If you know something about my son, you have to tell me —

DR. SWEET. They're watching us. If I say too much —

AGNES. Just tell me, he's alive, he's alive, and he's okay. *(Sweet nods.)* Oh, God, where is he? Just tell me where — *(Sweet puts a finger to his lips.)*

DR. SWEET. I have to be discreet. If I say too much, they might hurt him. You don't want that, do you? *(She shakes her head, weeping.)*

AGNES. *(To herself, under.)* He's alive, he's alive, he's alive, he's alive, he's alive —

DR. SWEET. Help me bring Peter in. And I'll help you find Lloyd … *(She nods. The bathroom door creaks open slowly and Peter steps into the room. His eyes look glassy and sick; his arms have been striated with cuts — droplets of blood ooze from the long slices and drip from his fingertips. He holds a butcher knife with a ten-inch blade. Agnes immediately goes to him; Sweet slowly retreats toward the door.)* Peter, good Lord —

AGNES. Lloyd's alive, he's alive … he says he'll give me Lloyd, and take care of you, help you, they'll take you in, cut out the egg sacs — *(Peter crosses to Sweet, who gingerly backs against the front door.)* Peter…?

DR. SWEET. Peter … *(Peter sniffs him … raises the knife … pokes*

46

gently at Sweet's belly.)

PETER. What are you?

AGNES. What are you doing?

DR. SWEET. You need to come back …

PETER. *(Sniffing.)* From the factory. Sound card's good. What do you run on?

DR. SWEET. You need your meds …

PETER. New model.

DR. SWEET. And we need to talk, talk to one another …

AGNES. Do you know who he is?

DR. SWEET. He knows me. It's all right.

PETER. Munitions, R and D, nice work.

AGNES. What's happening? *(Peter turns to Agnes.)*

PETER. You believed it.

DR. SWEET. She's not a part of this —

AGNES. He told me he'd help me find my son —

PETER. It'll tell you anything you want to hear.

DR. SWEET. This is between you and me, Peter —

PETER. That's how it's programmed.

AGNES. I don't understand.

DR. SWEET. It's always been you and me —

PETER. I'll cut it open. I'll show you. *(Sweet turns, desperately flails with the locks on the door. Peter sees him, flies at him. Just as Sweet gets the door open, Peter buries the knife blade under his ribs. Agnes screams, rushes Peter. Sweet struggles to get out the open door. Peter kicks it shut, repeatedly stabs Sweet, who stumbles backward. Agnes keeps screaming, trying to stop Peter's attack. He throws her off, returns to stabbing Sweet, again, again, again.)* Machine … machine … machine …

AGNES. He was going to help me find my son! *(Peter drops the knife, grabs Agnes, wrestles her over to Sweet's body.)*

PETER. Touch it! Here, feel it! *(He forces her to touch the body, put her hands in the blood.)* It isn't real!

AGNES. Real what?!

PETER. I have no idea what that is! *(He rubs his hands together, shows her.)* Synthetic … it's not even …

AGNES. He knew about my son!

PETER. It doesn't know anything! It knows what they've programmed it to say!

AGNES. I don't know what you're talking about! He said he knew about Lloyd!

PETER. They can't wait for me to go outside any more. They've come to collect me; their experiment is over and they've come to pick up their petri dish, and they've sent a machine to do it. Agnes, it's a fucking machine! You can see for yourself! They're sending in machines!

AGNES. I don't understand! Tell me what's going on!

PETER. You want to know what's going on? All right, then you listen to me, you listen to what I'm going to tell you, because you don't know the fucking enormity of what we're dealing with here —

AGNES. I'm listening —

PETER. May the twenty-ninth, 1954, a consortium of bankers, industrialists, corporate CEOs, and politicians held a series of meetings over three days at the Bilderberg Hotel in Oosterbeek, Holland. They drew up a plan for maintaining the status quo —

AGNES. What is that?

PETER. It's *the way things are*. It's the rich get richer, and the poor get poorer. It's a piece of shit, but you got to where you kind of liked it.

AGNES. All right —

PETER. They devised a plan to manipulate technology, economics, the media, population control, world religion, to keep things *the way they are*. They have continued to meet once a year, every year, since that original meeting. Look it up.

AGNES. Okay …

PETER. Under their orders, the CIA had smuggled Nazi scientists into the States to work with the American military at Calspan, developing an inner-epidermal tracking microchip —

AGNES. Wait —

PETER. — a surveillance tool, a computer chip implanted in the skin of every human being born on this planet since 1982. An early test group for the prototype was the Peoples Temple, and when the Reverend Jim Jones threatened to expose them, he and every member of his church were assassinated —

AGNES. Jesus, I —

PETER. — but it wasn't enough just to track people, to spy on them; they wanted control. They created the Intelligence Manned Interface biochip, a subcutaneous transponder, a computer chip imprinted with living brain cells. They needed lab rats to test it, and they found us: me, in the Gulf, and another soldier working at Calspan at the time: Tim McVeigh.

AGNES. Oh, no, wait —

48

PETER. They turned us into fucking zombies, remote control assassins, then picked Tim up, chucked him in a prison factory. But I found my chip and cut it out, so they sent me back to the lab for further testing and a new experiment.

AGNES. Wait a minute, you're John Doe number two.

PETER. No, that's who they want me to be. That's the flaw in the IMI biochip: They can't get to everybody, people slip through the cracks, or find the chip and remove it, like me, or Ted Kaczynski. They need a chip that will self-perpetuate, that will spread, like a virus, that people can pass to each other, to everyone.

AGNES. Okay …

PETER. They got it.

AGNES. They got it. What, they got the — ? The bugs? You mean the bugs — ?

PETER. A living, breathing organism; the ultimate parasite, implanted via a queen bug, the super-mother, who mates with a drone, lays egg sacs within the body of the host, and governs a growing army of rapidly multiplying brainwashing bugs.

AGNES. Jesus … they gave them to you … and you gave them to me, you gave those fuckin' things TO ME!

PETER. Maybe.

AGNES. Of course you did —

PETER. I don't believe my presence here is accidental.

AGNES. Y'think I had somethin' to do with this? Peter. I didn't know, I couldn'ta been a part of it. Unless I know somethin' I don't know I know, or I have somethin' I don't know I have —

PETER. What don't you know?

AGNES. A lot of things.

PETER. What don't you know?

AGNES. I, I —

PETER. Think, Agnes: What don't you know?

AGNES. Christ —

PETER. What one, very important thing don't you know?

AGNES. Lloyd.

PETER. What happened to Lloyd.

AGNES. I don't know.

PETER. You do know.

AGNES. I don't —

PETER. Put it together. The pieces fit.

AGNES. They won't. They won't fit.

PETER. You have to look hard enough. You'll see it.

49

AGNES. I can't see it.

PETER. Look harder.

AGNES. I don't see it. You have to help me. You have to help me see it.

PETER. You'll see it.

AGNES. I don't know how to start.

PETER. Start at the beginning.

AGNES. The beginning …

PETER. Lloyd.

AGNES. Uh … all right … he … he was with me, in the grocery store …

PETER. In the grocery store.

AGNES. In the cart … I forgot to get an onion … I went back for an onion, and left him in the cart … I came back to the cart, and he … he was just … he was gone …

PETER. He was "just" gone.

AGNES. He couldn'ta got out … not in that time, I was only gone a few seconds …

PETER. He couldn't have gotten out —

AGNES. He had to be took out … somebody had to take him out.

PETER. "Somebody."

AGNES. Not anyone. He didn't talk to strangers. I taught him not to talk to strangers, he knew, he was smart …

PETER. So then it had to be …

AGNES. Someone he knew … it had to be someone he knew … it had to be …

PETER. Who?

AGNES. It had to be … Goss. Goss had to take him … he woulda gone with Goss.

PETER. He would have gone with Goss.

AGNES. They couldn't help me, the police couldn't help me —

PETER. "Couldn't" help you —

AGNES. Wouldn't, they wouldn't help me. The FBI, they wouldn't help me. Nobody would help me.

PETER. *Why* wouldn't they help you?

AGNES. Because … they were in on it. They knew what Goss was doing, he took Lloyd, and they gave him to them, he gave Lloyd to them. They paid Goss for him, and he took him and gave him to them …

PETER. Get another piece.

AGNES. All right … you came here … you came, with R.C.

50

PETER. With R.C.

AGNES. Right. Right, R.C. brought you here. And, and now she's gone, she's gone because she … she was spying on you … she was spying on us …

PETER. Think.

AGNES. You brought the bugs … you have the bugs in your body, the egg sacs in your body.

PETER. I brought the bugs.

AGNES. And R.C. brought you. You brought the bugs, and R.C. brought you. R.C. brought the bugs.

PETER. Right.

AGNES. And Goss, Goss got out of prison … he got early parole, he wasn't supposed to get out … he got out, just when you showed up.

PETER. Just when I showed up.

AGNES. So he … he was …

PETER. He was what?

AGNES. He was …

PETER. What?

AGNES. Sent…? *(Peter nods. Now she's got it.)* He was sent here. They let him out, to send him here — he made a deal to get out, they let him out, sent him here to spy on us. Because of the bugs. To track the bugs, check their progress. And R.C. tried to tell us there weren't any bugs, but she brought the bugs. They made her bring the bugs to me. The kid, Lavoice's boy, they gave her Lavoice's boy, they never woulda done that, but she brought the bugs to me in exchange for Lavoice's son. *(Beat.)* Except you didn't have the bugs until you got here. They kept you, for all that time, but you didn't have bugs until after you came, after you, after we … oh my God, so, it's, we're, they're — it's us. They gave you the worker, the, the drone, but they gave me the queen. That's when they came out, that's when they mated, when we … when we … we made them. Us. And they needed me because I was, I was, I was the only one, because they took Lloyd, they took him, they took him to a lab somewheres, like this laboratory, and cut on him, cut him up, our stuff matched or whatever, our blood, our DNA, they planned it from the beginning, to take a kid, and cut him up, slice him up, on a table, and make the, the, build the, the queen to match up with the mother, they made the queen for me, for me, designed it for me, they gave me the mother, they gave me the queen, the juice, the bug, the mother, the bug, the super-mother, the super-mother bug, inside me. I'm the supermother. I'm the super-mother. I'm the supermother. And now that we made them, now that we gave birth to them, these people, they're coming in here, because the bugs won't leave, they won't do their work, until we're dead, because we made them, and they wouldn't leave us, they'd never leave us, we're all they know, we're all they've got, so they're coming in here, these people, to kill us, and send the bugs out, out into the world, the world. *(She collapses, weeps.)* My baby. *(Peter takes her in his arms, strokes her, holds her.)*

PETER. It's better. Knowing.

AGNES. Yes. *(Beat.)* We have to kill them.

PETER. Yes.

AGNES. We have a responsibility. *(A knock at the door. Peter and Agnes jump at the sound, quickly kill the lights. They wait. Another knock. Peter nods.)* Who is it?

PIZZA HARRIS. *(Offstage.)* Pizza Harris. *(Agnes and Peter look at each other.)*

AGNES. When did I order a pizza?

PETER. Did you order a pizza?

PIZZA HARRIS. *(Offstage.)* Pizza Harris. *(Beat.)* Hello?

AGNES. Just … leave it outside the door.

PIZZA HARRIS. *(Offstage.)* You gotta pay me, lady.

AGNES. How much is it?

PIZZA HARRIS. *(Offstage.)* Fourteen-seventy-five. *(She finds her purse, takes out her wallet.)*

PETER. What's on it?

PIZZA HARRIS. *(Offstage.)* Everything.

PETER. Everything?

PIZZA HARRIS. *(Offstage.)* Everything.

PETER. *(To himself.)* Everything.

AGNES. I'll just slide a twenty under the door.

PIZZA HARRIS. *(Offstage.)* You want change?

AGNES. NO! Just … take the twenty and go. *(Beat.)* Hello — ?

PIZZA HARRIS. *(Offstage.)* Yeah, whatever. *(She slides the twenty halfway under the door. She and Peter stare at the twenty as it zips away.)*

AGNES. Is he gone? *(Peter shrugs. To the door.)* Are you gone? *(She looks to Peter.)*

PETER. If we don't open the door, they'll know we know. *(She quickly opens the door, grabs the pizza, pulls it into the room, closes the door. She slides the pizza box between herself and Peter. They stare at it.)* Open it. *(She does, slowly.)* Hold it. *(He grabs the Exacto knife, slices*

off a bite, places it in a petri dish, and examines it under the microscope.)
AGNES. How does it look?
PETER. I'm no expert. *(She looks in the microscope.)*
AGNES. I don't think it's clean.
PETER. Vicious bastards … *(Scratching at the door. Agnes and Peter exchange a look, then quickly pull the mattress off the bed and move it in front of the door. The helicopter buzzes, quickly approaching. Peter goes for the box springs. The door opens a crack, held by the chain, the mattress, Agnes.)*

AGNES.	PETER.
Peter — !	Hold it —

(Goss's hand reaches through the door, fumbling for the chain.)

AGNES.	GOSS. *(Offstage.)*
They're coming in!	Aggie — !

PETER. They're not taking me out of here! *(Peter hauls the box springs to the door. The helicopter quickly grows to a tremendous roar.)*

AGNES.	GOSS. *(Offstage.)*
I can't hold it — !	Get away from the door!

PETER. NO AUTOPSY!

AGNES.	GOSS. *(Offstage.)*
Hurry — !	Aggie — !

(Agnes grabs the staple gun, shoots staples into Goss's hand. Goss screams, withdraws his hand. Agnes slams the door shut. Agnes and Peter wedge the box springs into place. Goss pounds on the door. Agnes and Peter look at the walls, the ceiling. Goss's pounding stops. The sound of the helicopter changes, mutates into the sound of a swarm of bugs.)
AGNES. Oh my God …
PETER. They're coming out.
AGNES. Oh God …
PETER. They're all coming out.
AGNES. Look … look at the ceiling …
PETER. … everywhere …
AGNES. … everywhere … *(Agnes and Peter uncork the jerry cans, throw gasoline on the walls, the floor, the bed, Dr. Sweet.)*
PETER. We'll fight them. To the end.
AGNES. You and me.
PETER. To the death.
AGNES. Our children. *(Noises cease. Peter drops the gas can. He and Agnes undress, watching the bugs swarm over their skin. They sit on the floor.)*
PETER. Find the drones … find the queen …

AGNES. Under the skin …
PETER. Breeding ground.
AGNES. Egg sac …
PETER. Larvae pool …
AGNES. Baby bug water …
PETER. Feeding pupa …
AGNES. Feeding bug baby …
PETER. Imago den …
AGNES. Skin ground breeding egg sac bugs …
PETER. I love you …
AGNES. I love you … *(He strikes a match. Blackout. Fire, buzzing.)*

End of Play

PROPERTY LIST

Pot of coffee, hot plate
Sheets, blanket, pillows
Bug spray, fly strips, flyswatter, roach motels
Children's toys, crayons, clothing
Tinfoil, staple gun
Stool covered with bedsheet
Cigarette, lighter (AGNES)
Wine glass (AGNES)
Waitress apron with money (AGNES)
Jug of loose change (AGNES)
Empty and full bottles of wine, corkscrew (AGNES)
Dirty dishes, dish soap (AGNES)
Lipstick (AGNES)
Freebase and crack pipe (AGNES, PETER, DR. SWEET)
Cocaine, razor blade (R.C.)
Dollar bill (R.C.)
Vial of cocaine (R.C.)
Coke (PETER)
Smoke alarm (PETER)
Pillow and blanket (AGNES)
Towel, coffee mug (GOSS)
Sack of muffins (PETER)
Purse with money (AGNES)
Suitcase (GOSS)
Wet washcloth, bottle of aspirin (PETER)
Vodka, cigarette (AGNES)
Clock radio (AGNES)
Chemistry set with microscope, petri dishes, glass slides,
    vials (PETER)
Exacto knife, petri dish, microscope (PETER)
Magnifying glass, pen and journal (PETER)
Lock pick (GOSS)
Toilet paper (GOSS)
Safety pin (PETER)
Purse with tube of ointment (PETER)
Coat hanger (PETER)
Blanket (AGNES)
Toolbox with pliers (PETER)
Tooth, microscope, petri dish (PETER)

Billfold (DR. SWEET)
Two five-gallon jerry cans (DR. SWEET, AGNES)
Petri dish (AGNES)
Notepad, pen (DR. SWEET)
Butcher knife (PETER)
Pizza (PIZZA HARRIS)
Purse, wallet, money (AGNES)
Exacto knife, petri dish, microscope (PETER)
Mattress, box springs (PETER)
Staple gun (AGNES)
Matches (PETER)

SOUND EFFECTS

Radio salsa music
Traffic
Phone ring
Air conditioner
Country-and-western music
Chirping
Garbage truck
Running shower
Helicopter
Argument
Knocking
Swarm of bugs
Fire, buzzing

NEW PLAYS

★ **GUARDIANS by Peter Morris.** In this unflinching look at war, a disgraced American soldier discloses the truth about Abu Ghraib prison, and a clever English journalist reveals how he faked a similar story for the London tabloids. "Compelling, sympathetic and powerful." *–NY Times.* "Sends you into a state of moral turbulence." *–Sunday Times (UK).* "Nothing short of remarkable." *–Village Voice.* [1M, 1W] ISBN: 978-0-8222-2177-7

★ **BLUE DOOR by Tanya Barfield.** Three generations of men (all played by one actor), from slavery through Black Power, challenge Lewis, a tenured professor of mathematics, to embark on a journey combining past and present. "A teasing flare for words." *–Village Voice.* "Unfailingly thought-provoking." *–LA Times.* "The play moves with the speed and logic of a dream." *–Seattle Weekly.* [2M] ISBN: 978-0-8222-2209-5

★ **THE INTELLIGENT DESIGN OF JENNY CHOW by Rolin Jones.** This irreverent "techno-comedy" chronicles one brilliant woman's quest to determine her heritage and face her fears with the help of her astounding creation called Jenny Chow. "Boldly imagined." *–NY Times.* "Fantastical and funny." *–Variety.* "Harvests many laughs and finally a few tears." *–LA Times.* [3M, 3W] ISBN: 978-0-8222-2071-8

★ **SOUVENIR by Stephen Temperley.** Florence Foster Jenkins, a wealthy society eccentric, suffers under the delusion that she is a great coloratura soprano—when in fact the opposite is true. "Hilarious and deeply touching. Incredibly moving and breathtaking." *–NY Daily News.* "A sweet love letter of a play." *–NY Times.* "Wildly funny. Completely charming." *–Star-Ledger.* [1M, 1W] ISBN: 978-0-8222-2157-9

★ **ICE GLEN by Joan Ackermann.** In this touching period comedy, a beautiful poetess dwells in idyllic obscurity on a Berkshire estate with a band of unlikely cohorts. "A beautifully written story of nature and change." *–Talkin' Broadway.* "A lovely play which will leave you with a lot to think about." *–CurtainUp.* "Funny, moving and witty." *–Metroland (Boston).* [4M, 3W] ISBN: 978-0-8222-2175-3

★ **THE LAST DAYS OF JUDAS ISCARIOT by Stephen Adly Guirgis.** Set in a time-bending, darkly comic world between heaven and hell, this play reexamines the plight and fate of the New Testament's most infamous sinner. "An unforced eloquence that finds the poetry in lowdown street talk." *–NY Times.* "A real jaw-dropper." *–Variety.* "An extraordinary play." *–Guardian (UK).* [10M, 5W] ISBN: 978-0-8222-2082-4

DRAMATISTS PLAY SERVICE, INC.
440 Park Avenue South, New York, NY 10016 212-683-8960 Fax 212-213-1539
postmaster@dramatists.com www.dramatists.com

NEW PLAYS

★ **THE GREAT AMERICAN TRAILER PARK MUSICAL music and lyrics by David Nehls, book by Betsy Kelso.** Pippi, a stripper on the run, has just moved into Armadillo Acres, wreaking havoc among the tenants of Florida's most exclusive trailer park. "Adultery, strippers, murderous ex-boyfriends, Costco and the Ice Capades. Undeniable fun." –*NY Post.* "Joyful and unashamedly vulgar." –*The New Yorker.* "Sparkles with treasure." –*New York Sun.* [2M, 5W] ISBN: 978-0-8222-2137-1

★ **MATCH by Stephen Belber.** When a young Seattle couple meet a prominent New York choreographer, they are led on a fraught journey that will change their lives forever. "Uproariously funny, deeply moving, enthralling theatre." –*NY Daily News.* "Prolific laughs and ear-to-ear smiles." –*NY Magazine.* [2M, 1W] ISBN: 978-0-8222-2020-6

★ **MR. MARMALADE by Noah Haidle.** Four-year-old Lucy's imaginary friend, Mr. Marmalade, doesn't have much time for her—not to mention he has a cocaine addiction and a penchant for pornography. "Alternately hilarious and heartbreaking." –*The New Yorker.* "A mature and accomplished play." –*LA Times.* "Scathingly observant comedy." –*Miami Herald.* [4M, 2W] ISBN: 978-0-8222-2142-5

★ **MOONLIGHT AND MAGNOLIAS by Ron Hutchinson.** Three men cloister themselves as they work tirelessly to reshape a screenplay that's just not working—*Gone with the Wind.* "Consumers of vintage Hollywood insider stories will eat up Hutchinson's diverting conjecture." –*Variety.* "A lot of fun." –*NY Post.* "A Hollywood dream-factory farce." –*Chicago Sun-Times.* [3M, 1W] ISBN: 978-0-8222-2084-8

★ **THE LEARNED LADIES OF PARK AVENUE by David Grimm, translated and freely adapted from Molière's *Les Femmes Savantes*.** Dicky wants to marry Betty, but her mother's plan is for Betty to wed a most pompous man. "A brave, brainy and barmy revision." –*Hartford Courant.* "A rare but welcome bird in contemporary theatre." –*New Haven Register.* "Roll over Cole Porter." –*Boston Globe.* [5M, 5W] ISBN: 978-0-8222-2135-7

★ **REGRETS ONLY by Paul Rudnick.** A sparkling comedy of Manhattan manners that explores the latest topics in marriage, friendships and squandered riches. "One of the funniest quip-meisters on the planet." –*NY Times.* "Precious moments of hilarity. Devastatingly accurate political and social satire." –*BackStage.* "Great fun." –*CurtainUp.* [3M, 3W] ISBN: 978-0-8222-2223-1

DRAMATISTS PLAY SERVICE, INC.
440 Park Avenue South, New York, NY 10016   212-683-8960   Fax 212-213-1539
postmaster@dramatists.com   www.dramatists.com

NEW PLAYS

★ **AFTER ASHLEY by Gina Gionfriddo.** A teenager is unwillingly thrust into the national spotlight when a family tragedy becomes talk-show fodder. "A work that virtually any audience would find accessible." –*NY Times.* "Deft characterization and caustic humor." –*NY Sun.* "A smart satirical drama." –*Variety.* [4M, 2W] ISBN: 978-0-8222-2099-2

★ **THE RUBY SUNRISE by Rinne Groff.** Twenty-five years after Ruby struggles to realize her dream of inventing the first television, her daughter faces similar battles of faith as she works to get Ruby's story told on network TV. "Measured and intelligent, optimistic yet clear-eyed." –*NY Magazine.* "Maintains an exciting sense of ingenuity." –*Village Voice.* "Sinuous theatrical flair." –*Broadway.com.* [3M, 4W] ISBN: 978-0-8222-2140-1

★ **MY NAME IS RACHEL CORRIE taken from the writings of Rachel Corrie, edited by Alan Rickman and Katharine Viner.** This solo piece tells the story of Rachel Corrie who was killed in Gaza by an Israeli bulldozer set to demolish a Palestinian home. "Heartbreaking urgency. An invigoratingly detailed portrait of a passionate idealist." –*NY Times.* "Deeply authentically human." –*USA Today.* "A stunning dramatization." –*CurtainUp.* [1W] ISBN: 978-0-8222-2222-4

★ **ALMOST, MAINE by John Cariani.** This charming midwinter night's dream of a play turns romantic clichés on their ear as it chronicles the painfully hilarious amorous adventures (and misadventures) of residents of a remote northern town that doesn't quite exist. "A whimsical approach to the joys and perils of romance." –*NY Times.* "Sweet, poignant and witty." –*NY Daily News.* "Aims for the heart by way of the funny bone." –*Star-Ledger.* [2M, 2W] ISBN: 978-0-8222-2156-2

★ **Mitch Albom's TUESDAYS WITH MORRIE by Jeffrey Hatcher and Mitch Albom, based on the book by Mitch Albom.** The true story of Brandeis University professor Morrie Schwartz and his relationship with his student Mitch Albom. "A touching, life-affirming, deeply emotional drama." –*NY Daily News.* "You'll laugh. You'll cry." –*Variety.* "Moving and powerful." –*NY Post.* [2M] ISBN: 978-0-8222-2188-3

★ **DOG SEES GOD: CONFESSIONS OF A TEENAGE BLOCKHEAD by Bert V. Royal.** An abused pianist and a pyromaniac ex-girlfriend contribute to the teen-angst of America's most hapless kid. "A welcome antidote to the notion that the *Peanuts* gang provides merely American cuteness." –*NY Times.* "Hysterically funny." –*NY Post.* "The *Peanuts* kids have finally come out of their shells." –*Time Out.* [4M, 4W] ISBN: 978-0-8222-2152-4

DRAMATISTS PLAY SERVICE, INC.
440 Park Avenue South, New York, NY 10016 212-683-8960 Fax 212-213-1539
postmaster@dramatists.com   www.dramatists.com

NEW PLAYS

★ **RABBIT HOLE by David Lindsay-Abaire.** Winner of the 2007 Pulitzer Prize. Becca and Howie Corbett have everything a couple could want until a life-shattering accident turns their world upside down. "An intensely emotional examination of grief, laced with wit." *–Variety.* "A transcendent and deeply affecting new play." *–Entertainment Weekly.* "Painstakingly beautiful." *–BackStage.* [2M, 3W] ISBN: 978-0-8222-2154-8

★ **DOUBT, A Parable by John Patrick Shanley.** Winner of the 2005 Pulitzer Prize and Tony Award. Sister Aloysius, a Bronx school principal, takes matters into her own hands when she suspects the young Father Flynn of improper relations with one of the male students. "All the elements come invigoratingly together like clockwork." *–Variety.* "Passionate, exquisite, important, engrossing." *–NY Newsday.* [1M, 3W] ISBN: 978-0-8222-2219-4

★ **THE PILLOWMAN by Martin McDonagh.** In an unnamed totalitarian state, an author of horrific children's stories discovers that someone has been making his stories come true. "A blindingly bright black comedy." *–NY Times.* "McDonagh's least forgiving, bravest play." *–Variety.* "Thoroughly startling and genuinely intimidating." *–Chicago Tribune.* [4M, 5 bit parts (2M, 1W, 1 boy, 1 girl)] ISBN: 978-0-8222-2100-5

★ **GREY GARDENS book by Doug Wright, music by Scott Frankel, lyrics by Michael Korie.** The hilarious and heartbreaking story of Big Edie and Little Edie Bouvier Beale, the eccentric aunt and cousin of Jacqueline Kennedy Onassis, once bright names on the social register who became East Hampton's most notorious recluses. "An experience no passionate theatergoer should miss." *–NY Times.* "A unique and unmissable musical." *–Rolling Stone.* [4M, 3W, 2 girls] ISBN: 978-0-8222-2181-4

★ **THE LITTLE DOG LAUGHED by Douglas Carter Beane.** Mitchell Green could make it big as the hot new leading man in Hollywood if Diane, his agent, could just keep him in the closet. "Devastatingly funny." *–NY Times.* "An out-and-out delight." *–NY Daily News.* "Full of wit and wisdom." *–NY Post.* [2M, 2W] ISBN: 978-0-8222-2226-2

★ **SHINING CITY by Conor McPherson.** A guilt-ridden man reaches out to a therapist after seeing the ghost of his recently deceased wife. "Haunting, inspired and glorious." *–NY Times.* "Simply breathtaking and astonishing." *–Time Out.* "A thoughtful, artful, absorbing new drama." *–Star-Ledger.* [3M, 1W] ISBN: 978-0-8222-2187-6

DRAMATISTS PLAY SERVICE, INC.
440 Park Avenue South, New York, NY 10016 212-683-8960 Fax 212-213-1539
postmaster@dramatists.com www.dramatists.com

3563268